ISBN 0 86163 090 4

Spring House, Spring Place
London NW 5, England
Printed in Hungary

Bible Stories for Children

Illustrated by Rene Cloke

AWARD PUBLICATIONS — LONDON

NOAH'S ARK

In the beginning God gave us the earth to be our home. But men soon forgot his goodness. They became greedy, cruel and selfish. All except Noah.

So God decided to renew the earth, to send floods to wash everything away. Only Noah and his family would be saved. So first Noah was told to build an ark, a big boat with three decks and a roof. He set to work with his sons. When the ark was ready they took their families aboard with two of every kind of bird and animal, as God directed. Then came rains so fierce, they covered the whole earth and the waters became as deep as the sea.

It rained for weeks and weeks but Noah's ark floated safely on. At last the deluge stopped and the waters began to recede. Noah sent out a dove to scout for dry land.

The bird soon returned for it had found nowhere to perch. So Noah knew the waters were still covering the trees and mountains. Later he sent the dove out again and this time it returned with an olive twig. So! The water was receding beneath the trees. Floods were leaving the land.

Soon they all left the ark to build fresh homes in this new and lovely world, washed clean. God blessed them and promised that never again would such floods cover the earth.

JACOB AND ESAU

In the land of Canaan there lived a man who had twin sons. His name was Isaac and he was very rich, owning large herds of sheep and other animals. When Isaac was very old and growing blind, he sent for the older twin whose name was Esau, to give him his blessing. Esau was out hunting, so Jacob the young twin pretended to be his brother. He put Esau's clothes on and covered his arms and neck with goatskin. Then he went to his father who, feeling his hairy arms and neck, thought he was Esau.

So Jacob received the blessing meant for Esau and no one could alter that. Esau was very angry and the whole family was upset. Isaac sent Jacob away to stay with relatives in a far off land, Haran.

JOSEPH

Jacob stayed in Haran for years and years. He married and had twelve sons and became even richer than his father. Esau forgave him later and he was able to take his family back to Canaan.

One of his sons was called Joseph and Jacob loved him best of them all. He gave Joseph a very special coat when he was quite young, which plainly showed he was his father's favourite. His older brothers worked very hard, herding sheep for their father. It was hurtful to see their little brother so favoured above themselves. Besides, Joseph was a tell-tale. He often carried stories about them to his father.

So the older brothers came to hate Joseph. When he told them about the dreams he had, in which they all bowed down to him, they hated him still more.

One day when they were herding sheep far off from home, they decided to put an end to this boy's tales and dreams. They stripped off his wonderful coat and put him down a dried-up well, intending to leave him there. Then they saw a camel-train passing that way and it gave one of the brothers a better idea. "Why don't we sell Joseph to those merchants," he said. "Then we need not leave him to die."

So it was arranged. Joseph was hauled up out of the well and sold to the merchants to be a slave in Egypt.

His master there was Potipher, commander of the King's guard. Joseph served him well and Potipher was pleased with him. However Potipher's wife hated Joseph. Although he now lived in Egypt, he still remembered the God of his own people. Potipher's wife tried to make him change his ways. When he refused, she had him put in jail.

Joseph was in prison a long time. He made friends and was put in charge of other prisoners by the chief jailer. Even there Joseph kept to the ways of his God and his people.

While he was there, he made a discovery. He found he could tell the meaning of dreams. He became well known for it. Even the King, the Pharaoh, came to hear of this prisoner who could interpret dreams.

So when Pharaoh had some strange dreams himself, about very thin cows and very fat cows, he sent for Joseph. The young prisoner saw the meaning of the dreams at once. There would be seven years of good harvests, he told Pharaoh, and then seven years of famine.

He advised Pharaoh to store all extra food gathered in during the years of plenty. Pharaoh, seeing he was clever and wise, made him Governor of Egypt, to be in charge of the stores for the whole country.

When the famine came, people travelled from miles away to buy food. Among them were Joseph's brothers, who came to buy corn. When they were brought into the presence of the Governor of Egypt, they did not for a moment think he might be their brother. Joseph did not tell them. He asked them instead to bring their youngest brother Benjamin to Egypt. They thought this very strange but did as he asked.

Then Joseph told them who he was and how very glad he was to see them all again. They were ashamed and sorry for what they had done to him but Joseph freely forgave them.

Then Pharaoh invited Jacob to come to Egypt, offering him good lands where he might settle with his family. Jacob came with all his people, happy and thankful to be with his beloved son he had thought was dead for so long.

MOSES

Jacob's family settled happily in Egypt. They married and had many children. They took care of their lands and grew rich. In time a new Pharaoh came to Egypt. He was afraid the Hebrew people would grow stronger than his own, so he ordered that all their baby boys should be thrown in the river.

One clever mother hid her baby among the river-reeds. Pharaoh's daughter found him there when she came to bathe. She called him Moses and said she would keep him as her own. So Moses grew up in a royal palace. Later God chose him to lead his people out of Egypt.

When they left, they took everything they had with them; animals, clothes, tents, gold and silver, everything. Pharaoh had agreed to this but then he changed his mind and sent his army after them. When they reached the sea, they thought they were trapped, with the sea before them and the chariots behind. Suddenly God parted the waters and they walked across on dry land.

The war-chariots followed but the sea, rushing in to its usual depth, engulfed them all. Then Moses and his people went on toward the land God had promised them.

They crossed mountains and deserts but God was always with them. When they ran out of food, he sent them quails and manna. When they had no water, he told Moses to strike a certain rock with his staff. Moses did it and water gushed out, enough for all to drink.

Then God called Moses to a high mountain. There he gave him laws, written by the finger of God on tablets of stone. These were the laws to be obeyed by God's own people.

Moses was away on the mountain for weeks. When he returned, he found the people worshipping a golden calf instead of God. They had melted down their golden rings to make it. Moses was so angry he threw the precious stones down and ordered the idol to be destroyed. Later he prayed that they might be forgiven. God forgave them, giving Moses the laws again, written on two new stones. We call these laws the ten Commandments.

SAMUEL, THE BOY IN THE TEMPLE

There was once a woman who longed to have a child of her own. She often prayed about this in the temple and God heard her prayers. At last she gave birth to a baby boy. She called him Samuel.

When Samuel was old enough, his mother and father took him to the temple with costly gifts to thank God for their child. Now he was going to serve in the temple and be taught by Eli the high priest.

There was a lot to learn but Samuel worked hard and became a great help to Eli. As he went on learning, he grew and sometimes his mother brought him a new coat or tunic.

One night the boy heard some one calling. He ran to Eli but the old priest said no, it was not he who called, but God. So when the call came again, Samuel listened carefully. He learned from God that Eli and his family would soon leave the temple. God had chosen Samuel to be his next high priest.

Samuel did become high priest and later was Judge over all Israel. As he grew older, the people wanted a king. With God's help Samuel first chose a man called Saul.

He was a good leader in battle but not a good king. So God told Samuel to find David, youngest son of Jesse. When Samuel found him, he was still a boy, minding his father's sheep. The old Judge knew, however, that he would later rule the people. He anointed him, pouring oil on his head, which was the sign of kingship.

David sometimes played cheerful music for King Saul when he was tired. But when the Philistines attacked Israel, Saul went away with his army to fight them. David was too young to be in the army but one day he took supplies to Saul's camp and from there he heard the Philistine champion daring *anyone* to come and fight him.

David said he could and Saul at first said, "No". Then, seeing how much the boy trusted God to care for him, he agreed to let him go.

The enemy champion was a giant. His name was Goliath. No one believed that this young lad could possibly withstand him. He came to battle with a sword and shield. David had only five small stones and a sling, the weapon used by shepherds. He took careful aim.

His first stone hit Goliath's forehead. The giant fell to the ground. When his people saw that he was dead, they were dismayed and fled. Saul's army chased them as far as the sea. So David became a hero and Israel was saved.

David became a great leader and when Saul died he was made King of Israel. He ruled his people well and so did his son, Solomon, after him. He was famous for his wisdom and for the wonderful temple he built in Jerusalem.

People came from far off, including the Queen of Sheba, to visit this great temple.

THE PROPHET ELIJAH

Elijah was a man of God. He trusted him and spent long hours in prayer. The king of the country at that time was Ahab, who had turned from God with his cruel wicked wife Jezebel. Elijah warned them that God was so displeased, he would send a severe drought to their land.

The king and queen were terribly angry and Elijah needed to hide from them. He was led to a rocky place where he could not be seen. There was water to drink from a little stream and God sent ravens, who took food to him every day.

The stream dried up and Elijah was sent to the house of a widow, who lived in Sidon with her son. When Elijah arrived, she had only enough food for one meal. Elijah told her not to worry, as God would care for them. She used all she had to make the meal. On the following day and many more days, she found that there was always enough to make another meal.

One day her son fell ill and he died. Seeing the widow's grief, Elijah took the boy to his room and cried to God who heard his prayers. Life came back to the boy and his mother was overjoyed.

DANIEL IN THE LION'S DEN

Daniel grew up in a foreign land but he was so clever and studious, the king there made him a high official. This caused bad feelings, especially as Daniel did not believe in the gods of the land. His enemies persuaded the king to pass a new law, saying everyone must pray to the king himself for thirty days.

But Daniel could only pray to his own God. So, much against his will, King Darius sent him to punishment in the lion-pit. He was there all night but he trusted in God and the lions did not harm him. When Darius found him safe and well, he brought him out of the pit, giving praise to Daniel's god and punishment to his enemies.

THE STORY OF JONAH

Jonah was chosen to go to the great city of Nineveh to tell its people that God was displeased with them. But Jonah was afraid to do it. He ran away instead and got on board a ship.

A raging storm overtook them and the sailors thought they would sink. Jonah confessed that the storm might be following *him,* so they threw him overboard. The ship sailed on, leaving Jonah miles from land. He was flung about by heavy seas and finally was swallowed by a whale. After three days, the big fish set him down on the shore.

Then Jonah knew what he must do. He went to Nineveh and gave God's message to the people. They mended their ways at once and so were saved from disaster.